WICKERSLEY

START-UP
GEOGRAPHY

OUR
LOCAL AREA

Anna Lee

Evans

Published by Evans Brothers Limited
2A Portman Mansions
Chiltern Street
London W1U 6NR

Reprinted 2006
Produced for Evans Brothers Limited by
White-Thomson Publishing Ltd.
2/3 St Andrew's Place
Lewes, East Sussex BN7 1UP

Printed in China by W K T Co. Ltd.

© Evans Brothers Limited 2003
Editor: Elaine Fuoco-Lang
Consultants: Lorraine Harrison, Senior Lecturer in
Geography Education at the University of Brighton
and Christine Bentall, Key Stage One teacher at
St Bartholomew's Church of England Primary
School, Brighton.
Designer: Tessa Barwick
Map artwork: The Map Studio

Cover: All photographs by Alan Towse

British Library Cataloguing in Publication Data
Lee, Anna
    Our Local area. - (Start-up geography)
    1.Local geography - Juvenile literature
    I.Title
    910

ISBN: 0 237 52461 9
13-digit ISBN (from 1 Jan 2007) 978 0 237 52461 6

Acknowledgements: The publishers would like to thank
the following for their involvement with this book:
staff, students and parents at Crampton Primary School,
Southwark, Market Lane Garage, Joseph Letang,
The Imperial War Museum, London

Picture Acknowledgements: All photographs by
Alan Towse except Corbis 11 (left); Bryan and Cherry
Alexander Photography 19.

Contents

Our school 4

Workplaces 6

Shopping 8

After school and at the weekend 10

Buildings in our area 12

Features of the area 14

Changes in our area 16

Our High Street today and in the past 18

A map of our area 20

Further information for Parents and Teachers 22

Index 24

Our school

tube station

▼ **This is the entrance to school. It is on a quiet road in the centre of a big city.**

Imperial War Museum

Crampton Primary School

market

gardens

There are many places to see in the area around our school.

quiet road   centre   places

► There are places where people live ...

▲ ... places where people shop ...
... places where people work ...

► ... and places where people play.

live   shop   work   play

5

Workplaces

Many people work in our local area.

▶ Karen's mum works in the factory that makes clothes.

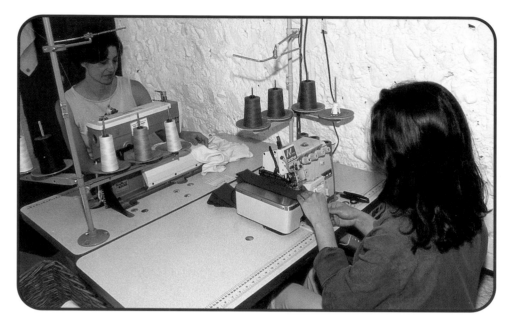

◀ Peter's dad works in the offices by the museum.

factory   offices   museum

◀ Mina's dad works in the garage next to the bank.

What places near your school do people work in?

garage   bank

Shopping

▶ **There is a big supermarket near our school.**

It sells all kinds of food.

Clare and Paul go shopping there with their mother.

▼ **There is a car park for customers.**

supermarket near car park

Jamie's dad walks to the smaller shops nearby.

There is a butcher, a baker and a greengrocer.

◀ Mina's mother likes talking to the stallholders at the market.

Where do your parents go shopping?

smaller   market

After school and at the weekend

◀ **Sometimes Peter, Karen and their friends go the leisure centre after school.**

▼ **Mina prefers to play in the playground at the park.**

What do you like to do after school?

leisure centre   playground

► **Jamie and his parents walk to church on Sundays.**

◄ **Mina goes to the mosque on Fridays.**

The mosque is a long way from our local area.

church   mosque

Buildings in our area

Here are some more buildings in our local area.

Can you tell which buildings are old and which are new?

restaurant

Imperial War Museum

library

post office

buildings

The things in the pictures on this page belong in one of the buildings on the opposite page.

Can you match the pictures with the buildings?

Features of the area

Our local area has many features other than buildings.

There is a park with a garden ...

... a railway bridge ...

... a war memorial ...   ... and a peace monument.

Use the words
at the bottom
of the page to
describe
these places.

quiet pretty dull ugly clean

This chart shows the feature members of our class like best.

Which is Jamie's favourite feature?

PEACE MONUMENT	RAILWAY BRIDGE	WAR MEMORIAL	PARK
Charmin	Robbie	Karen	Jamie
Jitesh	Paul	Jane	Marco
Peter	Maria	Mina	Sally
Clare	Pradniya	Steve	Elaine
	Kate		Vani
	Solomon		Enrico
	Carla		

chart   like   favourite

Changes in our area

Our local area is changing all the time.

What changes are taking place in these pictures?

changing

These people are doing things to improve the local area.

What else can we do to make our environment more attractive?

improve   environment   attractive   **17**

Our High Street today

Here are two pictures of a **street** near our school.

This photograph was taken this year ...

street

and in the past

... and this photograph was taken when our parents were young.

Can you spot the **differences** between the two?

differences

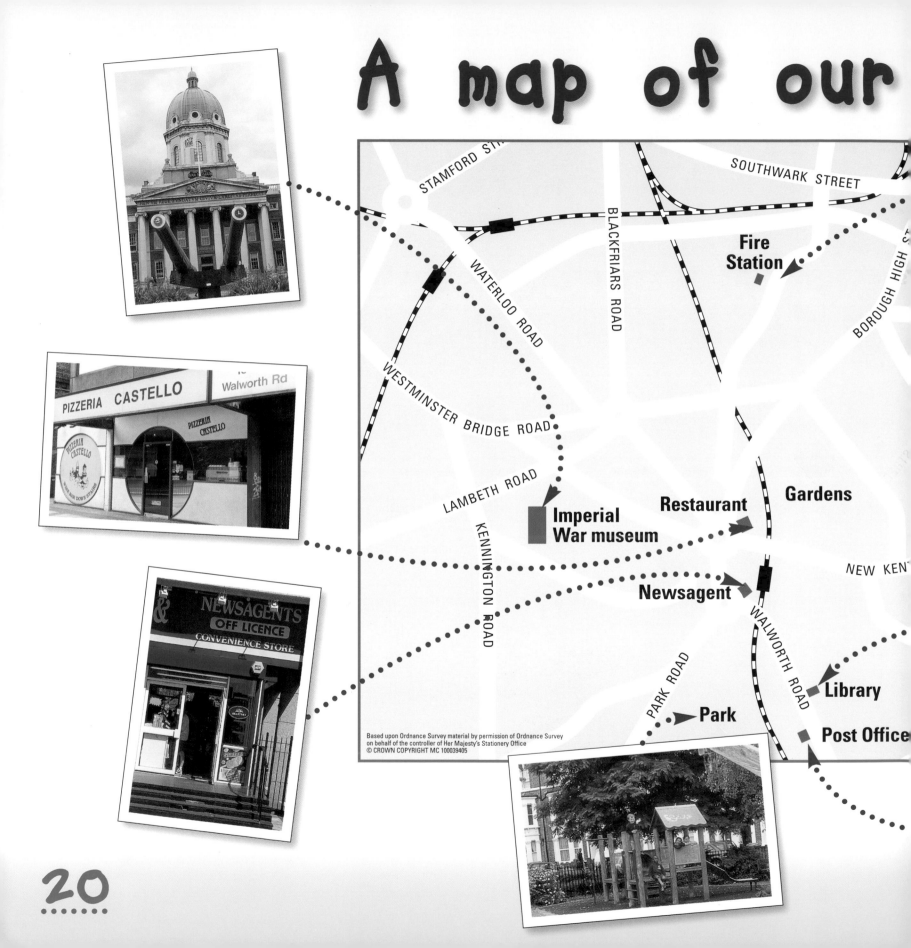

STAMFORD STREET

SOUTHWARK STREET

BLACKFRIARS ROAD

BOROUGH HIGH ST

**Fire
Station**

WATERLOO ROAD

WESTMINSTER BRIDGE ROAD

LAMBETH ROAD

Restaurant

Gardens

**Imperial
War museum**

KENNINGTON ROAD

NEW KENT

Newsagent

WALWORTH ROAD

PARK ROAD

▶ **Park**

Library

Post Office

Based upon Ordnance Survey material by permission of Ordnance Survey
on behalf of the controller of Her Majesty's Stationery Office
© CROWN COPYRIGHT MC 100039405

PIZZERIA CASTELLO
Walworth Rd

NEWSAGENTS
OFF LICENCE
CONVENIENCE STORE

area

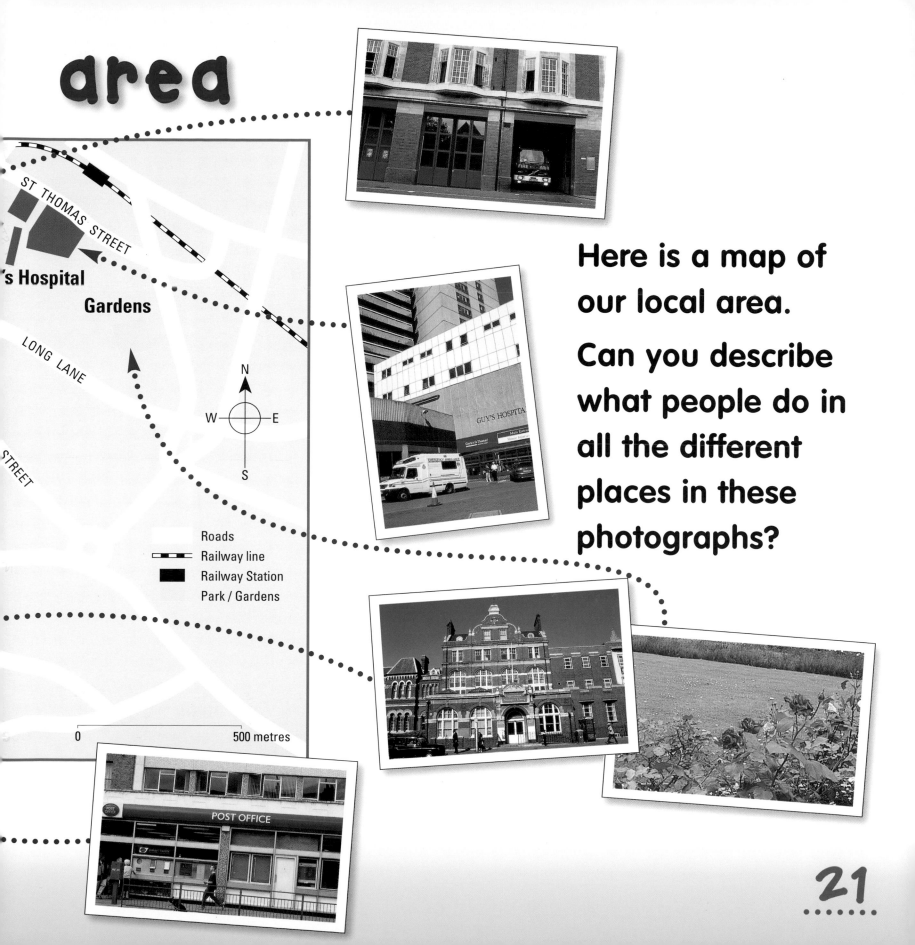

ST THOMAS STREET

's Hospital

Gardens

LONG LANE

STREET

N
W—E
S

Roads
Railway line
Railway Station
Park / Gardens

0   500 metres

POST OFFICE

GUY'S HOSPITAL

Here is a map of our local area.

Can you describe what people do in all the different places in these photographs?

Further information for

New words listed in the text:

attractive	chart	factory	live	places	shop
bank	church	favourite	market	play	smaller
buildings	clean	garage	mosque	playground	street
car park	differences	improve	museum	pretty	supermarket
centre	dull	leisure centre	near	quiet	ugly
changing	environment	like	offices	quiet road	work

Possible Activities

SPREAD ONE

Locate your school on a map and mark on it places of interest in the local area.

Mark on a map of the local area the places where the children live.

SPREAD TWO

Conduct a survey to show the types of jobs that parents/carers do.

Plot on a bar graph the types of places where parents/carers and family and friends work.

Ask local business people to come in and talk about their jobs.

SPREAD THREE

On a large scale map locate and name shops in the local area or the nearest town/village.

Visit a supermarket or the local shops and buy ingredients for a stew, salad or playtime snacks.

List different types of shops and write about the things they sell. Draw the items listed.

SPREAD FOUR

Make a graph of 'out of school activities' to see which is the most popular.

Visit different types of churches in the area.

Ask a local religious leader or parents to come into the school to talk about their religion.

Collect and display artefacts from different religions.

Make a 3D playground.

Parents and Teachers

SPREAD FIVE

Make a tourist guide to your local area using a computer and a digital camera.

Look at the places in your local area and draw a picture of something you would associate with it, for example with a bank you would associate money, a garage you would associate cars etc.

SPREAD SIX

Make a list of your favourite places and plot them on a graph.

SPREAD SEVEN

What changes have/are happening in your local area?

Brainstorm how you might change a part of your school or a place close by.

Write a letter to the local council asking them for extra rubbish bins or recycling centres.

Set up an anti-litter club.

SPREAD EIGHT

Collect pictures/postcards/objects of things past and present on the same subject, for example a candle and a lamp, an old teddy and a new teddy.

Compare and contrast the collection of objects.

SPREAD NINE

Set up a class post office, museum or hospital, in the classroom.

Further Information

BOOKS

FOR CHILDREN

Places We Share by Sally Hewitt (Franklin Watts 2000)
Shopping by Sally Hewitt (Franklin Watts 2000)
Street by Sally Hewitt (Franklin Watts 2000)
Where We Live by Sally Hewitt (Franklin Watts 2000)
Homes by Jeff Stanfield (Hodder Wayland 1999)
Shops by Jeff Stanfield (Hodder Wayland 1999)
The Street by Jeff Stanfield (Hodder Wayland 1999)

FOR ADULTS

Handbook of Primary Geography by Roger Carter (Ed) (The Geographical Association 1998)
Also refer to local area guide books and Ordnance Survey maps

WEBSITES

http://www.local-transport.dft.gov.uk/schooltravel/safe/index.htm
http://www.standards.dfee.gov.uk/schemes/geography
http://www.streetmap.co.uk
http://learn.co.uk

Index

b
bank 7
bridge 14
buildings 12-13

c
car park 8
changes 16-17
church 11
city centre 4

e
environment 17

f
factory 6
features 14-15

g
garage 7

i
Imperial War Museum 12
improvements 17

l
leisure centre 10
library 12

m
map 20-21
market 9
monument 14
mosque 11
museum 6, 12

o
offices 6

p
park 14

peace monument 14
play 5
playground 10
post office 12

q
quiet roads 4

r
railway bridge 14
restaurant 12

s
shopping 5, 8-9
street 18-19
supermarket 8

w
war memorial 14
workplaces 5, 6-7